CHRISTMAS

CHRISTMAS

An Illustrated Treasury

Compiled by Michelle Lovric

COURAGE BOOKS

an imprint of
RUNNING PRESS
Philadelphia • London

Copyright © 1994 by Royle Publications Limited
Royle House
Wenlock Road
London N1 7ST
England

Concept developed by Michelle Lovric
53 Shelton Street
Covent Garden
London WC2H 9HE
England

Canadian representatives: General Publishing Co., Ltd.,
30 Lesmill Road, Don Mills, Ontario M3B 2T6.

9 8 7 6 5 4 3 2 1
Digit on the right indicates the number of this printing.

Library of Congress Cataloging-in-Publication Number 93–74699

ISBN 1–56138–437–2

Cover design by Toby Schmidt
Cover illustration by Viggo Johansen
Interior design by Paul Kepple
Edited by Melissa Stein
Typography by Deborah Lugar

Running Press Book Publishers
125 South Twenty-second Street
Philadelphia, Pennsylvania 19103–4399

The author gratefully acknowledges the permission of the following to reproduce copyrighted material in this book:

P. 7 : From "Calendarium" from *Watching the Perseids* by Peter Scupham, published by Oxford University Press. Copyright © 1990 by Peter Scupham.

P. 11: From *A Christmas Book* by Elizabeth Goudge, first published in Great Britain in 1967 by Hodder and Stoughton. Copyright © 1967 by Elizabeth Goudge.

P. 12: From *Christmas with Stephen Leacock, Reflections on the Yuletide Season*, by Stephen Leacock, published by Natural Heritage/Natural History Inc. Copyright © 1988 by Natural Heritage/Natural History Inc. and the Leacock Memorial Home.

P. 12: From "The Holly" by Walter de la Mare, courtesy of the Literary Trustees of Walter de la Mare and the Society of Authors as their representative.

P. 17 From *Cider with Rosie* by Laurie Lee, first published by The Hogarth Press. Copyright © 1959 by Laurie Lee.

P. 18: From *Open Heavens, Meditations for Advent and Christmas*, by Eugen Drewermann, translated by David J. Kreiger, published by Orbis Books, New York. English translation copyright © 1991 by Orbis Books. Originally published in Germany by Patmos Verlag. Copyright © 1990 by Patmos Verlag.

P. 20: Quotation by Jane T. Clement from *Behold the Star, A Christmas Anthology*, edited by The Society of Brothers, published by the Plough Publishing House of The Hutterian Brethren Service Committee, Farmington. Copyright © 1966/67 by the Plough Publishing House.

P. 25: From *Christmas* by William Sansom, published by Weidenfeld & Nicolson. Copyright © 1968 by William Sansom.

P. 27: From *The Rainbow* by D. H. Lawrence, pulbished by Penguin Books, New York, in 1917. Reprinted by permission of Laurence Pollinger Ltd. and the Estate of Frieda Lawrence Ravagli.

P. 28: From *The Homecoming, A Novel about Spencer's Mountain*, by Earl Hamner, Junior, published by Random House, Inc., New York. Copyright © 1979 by Earl Hamner, Junior.

P. 29: From "little tree" by e.e. cummings, from *e.e. cummings: Complete Poems 1904–1962*, published by W.W. Norton & Company Ltd. Copyright © 1976 by the Trustees for the e. e. cummings Trust. Reprinted with the permission of W.W. Norton & Company and Liveright Publishing Corporation.

P. 31: From "The Christmas Tree" by C. Day Lewis, from *The Complete Poems*, published by Sinclair Stevenson Ltd. Copyright © 1992 by The Estate of C. Day Lewis.

P. 34: From "To a Grandchild" from *A Christmas Sequence* by John V. Taylor, published by the Amate Press. Copyright © 1989 by John V. Taylor.

P. 35: From "A Gift from the Stars" by John Rice, reprinted by permission of the author. Copyright © 1988 by John Rice.

P. 38: From "Epstein, Spare that Yule Log," by Ogden Nash from *Collected Verse from 1929 on*, published by J. M. Dent & Sons in 1966. Copyright © 1966 by Ogden Nash, reprinted by permission of Curtis Brown Ltd.

P. 40: From "Poem for Christmas Day" from *A Blue Harvester Mug and Other Poems* by Kathleen Norcross, published by the Birmingham and Midland Institute. Copyright © 1990 by Kathleen Norcross.

P. 44: From the poem by Stephanie June Sorréll, reprinted by permission of the author.

I

CHRISTMAS IS A PAGEANT OF COLOR: THE RED OF HOLLY BERRIES, THE BRIGHT WRAPPINGS OF GIFTS, NOSES AND CHEEKS ROSY IN THE COLD, AND THE WHITENESS OF MUCH-HOPED-FOR SNOW, BLANKETING THE WORLD IN QUIET SOFTNESS. THE FRAGRANCE OF FIR TREES AND THE SOUNDS OF CAROLS WAFT UPON THE COLD NIGHT AIR, AND CHRISTMAS GLOWS WITH MERRIMENT AND GAIETY.

CHRISTMAS BEGAN WITH A FAMILY, AND THIS FESTIVAL OF LIGHT AND LIFE IS A TIME OF REUNION, REBIRTH, AND RENEWAL. THE HOLIDAY SEASON BRINGS A DESIRE TO ACT LOVINGLY, GIVE UNSTINTINGLY, AND RECEIVE GRACEFULLY. WE REENACT THE CHRISTMAS STORY IN OUR OWN WAYS. LIKE THE THREE KINGS, WE BESTOW GIFTS. THE LIGHT OF THAT BRIGHT CHRISTMAS STAR FLICKERS IN OUR CANDLES. AND LIKE THE SHEPHERDS, WE GATHER TOGETHER TO BEHOLD A MIRACLE AND SHARE IN THE WARMTH OF ITS GLORY.

HERE WE PRESENT TO YOU JOYOUS WORDS AND IMAGES OF CHRISTMASES PAST AND PRESENT, IN A TREASURY FOR THIS MOST BLESSED SEASON.

ove was born at Christmas.

CHRISTINA ROSSETTI (1830–1894)
ENGLISH POET

Daylight shortens; your anticipation

Eases the candle-flame towards the end.

Cassiopeia swings above the fir-trees,

Embraces night. Between such diagrams

Manger and child float down the centuries,

Brilliants nursed on soft cloth. Time is now:

Each life an altar where the Mystery

Repeats its dream of gift and sacrifice.

"December"
Peter Scupham, b. 1933
English writer and lecturer

THERE SEEMS A MAGIC IN THE VERY NAME OF CHRISTMAS.

Charles Dickens (1813–1870)
English writer

Christmas comes! He comes, he comes,

Ushered in with rain of plums;

Hollies in the window greet him;

Schools come driving past to meet him;

Gifts precede him, bells proclaim him,

Every mouth delights to name him. . . .

LEIGH HUNT (1784–1849)
ENGLISH WRITER AND POET

CHRISTMAS WAS THE PINNACLE OF OUR WINTER DELIGHT.

Winifred Foley, b. 1916
English writer

Snow lay on the croft and river-bank in undulations softer than the limbs of infancy. . . . But old Christmas smiled as he laid this cruel-seeming spell on the out-door world, for he meant to light up home with new brightness, to deepen all the richness of in-door colour, and give a keener edge of delight to the warm fragrance of food: he meant to prepare a sweet imprisonment that would strengthen the primitive fellowship of kindred, and make the sunshine of familiar human faces as welcome as the hidden day-star.

George Eliot [Mary Ann Evans] (1819–1880)
English writer

In the mid-winter gloom Christmas comes up over the horizon like a lighted ship homeward bound.

ELIZABETH GOUDGE (1900–1984)
ENGLISH WRITER

Christmas has always seemed . . . a day of enchantment, and the world about us on Christmas day, for one brief hour an enchanted world. On Christmas morning the streets are always bright with snow, not too much of it nor too little, hard-frozen snow, all crystals and glittering in the flood of sunshine that goes with Christmas day. . . . If there was ever any other Christmas weather I have forgotten it. . . . Only the memory of the good remains.

Stephen Leacock (1869–1944)
English-born Canadian humorist

WHEN HITHER, THITHER, FALLS THE SNOW,

AND BLAZES SMALL THE FROST,

NAKED AMID THE WINTER STARS

THE ELM'S VAST BOUGHS ARE TOSSED.

BUT O, OF ALL THAT SUMMER SHOWED

WHAT NOW TO WINTER'S TRUE

AS THE PRICKLE-BERIBBED DARK HOLLY TREE,

WITH ITS BERRIES BURNING THROUGH!

Walter de la Mare (1873–1956)
English poet and writer

CALM ON THE LISTENING EAR OF NIGHT

COME HEAV'N'S MELODIOUS STRAINS,

WHERE WILD JUDEA STRETCHES FAR

HER SILVER-MANTLED PLAINS

LIGHT ON THY HILLS, JERUSALEM!

THE SAVIOUR NOW IS BORN:

MORE BRIGHT ON BETHLEHEM'S JOYOUS PLAINS

BREAKS THE FIRST CHRISTMAS MORN.

"Calm on the Listening Ear of Night"
Edmund H. Sears (1810–1876)
American clergyman

fifteen

And two thousand Christmases became real to us then; the houses, the halls, the places of paradise had all been visited; the stars were bright to guide the Kings through the snow; and across the farmyard we could hear the beasts in their stalls. We were given roast apples and hot mince-pies, in our nostrils were spices like myrrh, and in our wooden box, as we headed back for the village, there were golden gifts for all.

Laurie Lee, b. 1914
English writer

I salute you! There is nothing I can give you which you have not; but there is much, that, while I cannot give, you can take.

No heaven can come to us unless our hearts find rest in it today. Take Heaven.

No peace lies in the future which is not hidden in this present instant. Take Peace.

The gloom of the world is but a shadow; behind it, yet, within our reach, is joy. Take Joy.

And so, at this Christmas time, I greet you, with the prayer that for you, now and forever, the day breaks and the shadows flee away.

ATTRIBUTED TO FRA GIOVANNI, 16TH–CENTURY ITALIAN PRIEST

ON NO OTHER DAY IN THE YEAR DO WE EXPERIENCE SUCH A DEEP LONGING

FOR PEACE AND SECURITY AS ON CHRISTMAS EVE. FOR ON THAT DAY OUR

MEMORIES GO FAR BACK INTO OUR OWN CHILDHOOD, TO THE TIME WHEN WE

EXPERIENCED PEACE AND SECURITY OURSELVES, OR AT LEAST HOPED FOR IT.

THEREFORE, DURING THE CHRISTMAS SEASON WE TRY HARD TO TELL THE PEOPLE

NEAR TO US HOW MUCH WE LOVE THEM, AND WE SINCERELY ASK THEM ALSO TO

LOVE US. . . . BECAUSE OF THIS WE MAKE A GREAT EFFORT TO BE WORTHY OF LOVE.

Eugen Drewermann, b. 1940
German pastor and psychologist

Some say that ever 'gainst the season comes

Wherein our Saviour's birth is celebrated

The bird of dawning singeth all night long;

and then, they say, no spirit dare stir abroad,

The nights are wholesome, then no planets strike,

No fairy takes, nor witch hath power to charm,

So hallow'd and gracious is the time.

WILLIAM SHAKESPEARE (1564–1616)
ENGLISH POET AND DRAMATIST

Christmas is a time of promise, the meaning of which man has never fully grasped; the joy of it is too deep for our small hearts, the message too simple and enormous to be simply believed, except by children.

JANE T. CLEMENT, B. 1917
AMERICAN MEMBER OF RELIGIOUS ORDER

Were I a philosopher, I should write
a philosophy of toys, showing that
nothing else in life needs to be taken
seriously, and that Christmas Day in
the company of children is one of the
few occasions on which men become
entirely alive.

ROBERT LYND (1892–1970)
AMERICAN SOCIOLOGIST

Yes, Virginia, there is a Santa Claus. He exists as certainly as love and generosity and devotion exist, and you know that they abound and give to your life its highest beauty and joy. Alas! How dreary would be the world if there were no Santa Claus! It would be as dreary as if there were no Virginias. There would be no childlike faith then, no poetry, no romance to make tolerable this existence. We should have no enjoyment, except in sense and sight. The eternal light with which childhood fills the world would be extinguished.

Not believe in Santa Claus! You might as well not believe in fairies!

Francis P. Church (1839–1906)
American journalist

WAS THERE EVER A WIDER AND MORE
LOVING CONSPIRACY THAN THAT WHICH
KEEPS THE VENERABLE FIGURE OF
SANTA CLAUS FROM SLIPPING AWAY,
WITH ALL THE OTHER OLD-TIME
MYTHS, INTO THE FORSAKEN
WONDERLAND OF THE PAST?

Hamilton Wright Mabie (1845–1916)
American editor and critic

. . . of all the beasts that begged to do him service, Claus liked the reindeer best. "You shall go with me in my travels, for henceforth I shall bear my treasures not only to the children of the North, but to the children in every land whither the star points me and where the cross is lifted up!" So said Claus to the reindeer, and the reindeer neighed joyously and stamped their hoofs impatiently, as though they longed to start immediately.

EUGENE FIELD (1850–1895)
AMERICAN WRITER

HAVE YOU SEEN GOD'S CHRISTMAS

TREE IN THE SKY,

WITH ITS TRILLIONS OF TAPERS

BLAZING HIGH?

Angela Morgan [Lauran Paine], b. 1916
American writer

What is the colour of Christmas?

Red? The red of toyshops on a dark winter's afternoon, of Father Christmas and the robin's breast?

Or green? Green of holly and spruce and mistletoe in the house, dark shadow of summer in leafless winter?

One might plainly add a romance of white, fields of frost and snow; thus white, green, red. . . .

But many will say that the significant color is gold, gold of fire and treasure, of light in the winter dark. . . .

WILLIAM SANSOM (1912–1976)
ENGLISH WRITER

IT IS, INDEED, THE SEASON OF
REGENERATED FEELING—THE SEASON
FOR KINDLING NOT MERELY THE FIRE
OF HOSPITALITY IN THE HALL, BUT THE
GENIAL FLAME OF CHARITY IN THE HEART.

Washington Irving (1783–1859)
American writer

The expectation grew more tense. The star was risen into the sky, the songs, the carols were ready to hail it. The star was the sign in the sky. Earth too should give a sign. As evening drew on, hearts beat fast with anticipation, hands were full of ready gifts. There were the tremulously expectant words of the church service, the night was past and the morning was come, the gifts were given and received, joy and peace made a flapping of wings in each heart, there was a great burst of carols, the Peace of the World had dawned, strife had passed away, every hand was linked in hand, every heart was singing.

D. H. Lawrence (1885–1930)
English writer

*I*nto the house the tree brought with it the memory of thousands of white-hot summer suns, the long wilderness of silence of snowmantled winters, the crash of thunderous storms, the softness of a new green spring, and all the wild things which had rested in its shade or nestled in its branches.

EARL HAMNER, JR.
20TH-CENTURY AMERICAN WRITER

little tree

little silent Christmas tree

you are so little

you are more like a flower

who found you in the green forest

and were you very sorry to come away?

see   i will comfort you

because you smell so sweetly. . . .

look   the spangles

that sleep all the year in a dark box

dreaming of being taken out and allowed to shine,

the balls the chains red and gold the fluffy threads,

put up your little arms

and i'll give them all to you to hold

every finger shall have its ring

and there won't be a single place dark or unhappy

e. e. cummings (1894–1962)
American poet

On one branch they hung little nets, cut out of colored paper; every net was filled with sweetmeats; golden apples and walnuts hung down, as if they grew there, and more than a hundred little candles, red, white and blue, were fastened to the different boughs. Dolls that looked exactly like real people—the Tree had never seen such before—swung among the foliage, and high on the summit of the Tree was fixed a tinsel star. It was splendid, particularly splendid.

Hans Christian Andersen (1805–1875)
Danish writer

Put out the lights now!
Look at the Tree, the rough tree dazzled
In oriole plumes of flame,
Tinselled with twinkling frost fire,
tasselled
With stars and moons—the same
That yesterday hid in the spinney
and had no fame
Till we put out the lights now.

C. Day Lewis (1904–1972)
Anglo-Irish poet

The Grocers'! oh the Grocers'! nearly closed, with perhaps two shutters down, or one; but through those gaps such glimpses! It was not alone that the scales descending on the counter made a merry sound, or that the twine and roller parted company so briskly, or that the canisters were rattled up and down like juggling tricks, or even that the blended scents of the tea and coffee were so grateful to the nose, or even that the raisins were so plentiful and rare, the almonds so extremely white, the sticks of cinnamon so long and straight, the other spices so delicious, the candied fruits so caked and spotted with molten sugar as to make the coldest looker-on feel faint and subsequently bilious. Nor was it that the figs were moist and pulpy, or that the French plums blushed in modest tartness from their highly-decorated boxes, or that everything was good to eat and in its Christmas dress; but the hopeful customers were all so hurried and so eager in the hopeful promise of the day, that they tumbled up against each other at the door, crashing their wicker baskets wildly, and left their purchases upon the counter, and came running back to fetch them, and committed hundreds of little mistakes, in the best humor possible. . . .

Charles Dickens (1812–1870)
English writer

Look beneath the tinsel for the treasure. . . . Christmas is a Baby and His parents. Christmas is a promise. It is looking back into times gone by and forward into days to come. . . . Christmas is an urge to give, to do, to be.

Faith Baldwin (1893–1978)
American writer

Over the swinging parapet of my arm

your sentinel eyes lean gazing. Hugely alert

in the pale unfinished clay of your infant face,

they drink the light from this candle on the tree.

Drinking, not pondering, each bright thing you

      see, you make it yours without analysis

and, stopping down the aperture of thought to a

      fine pinhole, you are filled with flame.

Give me for Christmas, then, your kind of seeing,

not studying candles—angel, manger, star—

but staring as at a portrait, God's I guess,

that shocks and holds the eye, till all my being,

gathered, intent and still, as now you are,

breathes out its wonder in a wordless yes.

JOHN V. TAYLOR, B. 1914
ENGLISH TEACHER AND WRITER, FORMER BISHOP OF WINCHESTER

. . . THE SECOND YOU OPEN YOUR EYES ON CHRISTMAS MORN

THE PARCEL BURSTS OPEN WITHOUT A SOUND

AND SHOWERS YOU WITH FROSTY STARS

THAT ZING AND SPIN AND MELT AND SPLIT AND VANISH

TO BECOME MINISCULE MOLECULES OF HAPPINESS.

John Rice, b. 1948
Scottish writer

. . . it was always a gamble
whether we would wake up and be
running downstairs before our
parents had gone to bed.

PAUL ENGLE, B. 1908
AMERICAN WRITER

Ah, what a beautiful morning. . . .

Everyone had dreamt of his dear ones that night,

In some strange dream where you could see toys,

Sweets covered with gold, sparkling jewels,

All whirling and dancing an echoing dance,

And then disappearing beneath the curtains, and then reappearing!

You awoke in the morning and got up full of joy,

With your mouth watering, rubbing your eyes. . . .

You went with tangled hair

And shining eyes, as on holiday mornings,

Little bare feet brushing the floor,

To tap softly on your parents' door. . . .

You went in! . . . And then came the greetings . . . in your nightshirt,

Kisses upon kisses, and fun all allowed!

ARTHUR RIMBAUD (1854–1891)
FRENCH WRITER

THERE WAS A GOOD DEAL OF LAUGHING
AND KISSING AND EXPLAINING, IN THE
SIMPLE, LOVING FASHION WHICH MAKES
THESE HOME FESTIVALS SO PLEASANT AT
THE TIME, SO SWEET TO REMEMBER
LONG AFTERWARDS. . . .

Louisa May Alcott (1832–1888)
American writer

How beautifully it steams! How delicious it smells! How round it is! A kiss is round, the horizon is round, the earth is round, the moon is round, the sun and stars and all the host of heavens are round. So is plum pudding.

THE ILLUSTRATED LONDON NEWS, DECEMBER 1848

Oh, give me an old-fashioned Christmas card,

With hostler hostling in an old inn yard,

With church bells chiming their silver notes,

And jolly red squires in their jolly red coats,

And a good fat goose by the fire that dangles,

And a few more angels and a few less angles.

Turn backward, Time, to please this bard,

And give me an old-fashioned Christmas card.

Ogden Nash (1902–1971)
American writer

GOOD NEWS: BUT IF YOU ASK ME WHAT IT IS, I KNOW NOT;

IT IS A TRACK OF FEET IN THE SNOW,

IT IS A LANTERN SHOWING A PATH,

IT IS A DOOR SET OPEN.

"Xmas Day"
G. K. Chesterton (1874–1936)
English writer

These are the Christmas joys I wish for you:
Sacrament, first, to greet the new-born Word;
Red sky and robins; noon an egg-shell blue;
At least one moment, when the air is stirred
By angels' wings. . . .
But these, like bulbs one plants, and does not say,
Whose stems stand hidden, in the frozen drifts,
Shall be my secret, love, till Christmas Day.

Kathleen Norcross, b. 1928
English writer

CHRISTMAS IS NOT A TIME OR A SEASON, BUT A STATE OF MIND. . . . TO CHERISH PEACE AND GOOD WILL, TO BE PLENTEOUS IN MERCY, IS TO HAVE THE REAL SPIRIT OF CHRISTMAS. IF WE THINK ON THESE THINGS, THERE WILL BE BORN IN US A SAVIOUR AND OVER US WILL SHINE A STAR SENDING ITS GLEAM OF HOPE TO THE WORLD.

Calvin Coolidge (1872–1933)
30th U.S. president

*I hold it as a memory of Heaven's
love and the world's peace.*

NICHOLAS BRETON (1533?–1625)
ENGLISH WRITER

I heard the bells on Christmas Day

Their old familiar carols play,

And wild and sweet

The word repeat

Of peace on earth, good will to men!

*Henry Wadsworth Longfellow (1807–1882)
American writer*

CHRISTMAS IS TRULY THE UNIVERSAL HOLIDAY OF ALL MEN. IT IS THE DAY WHEN ALL OF US DEDICATE OUR THOUGHTS TO OTHERS; WHEN ALL ARE REMINDED THAT MERCY AND COMPASSION ARE THE ENDURING VIRTUES; WHEN ALL SHOW, BY SMALL DEEDS AND LARGE AND BY ACTS, THAT IT IS MORE BLESSED TO GIVE THAN TO RECEIVE.

John F. Kennedy (1917–1963)
35th U.S. President

I greet you, dear friend
at this great festival of light.
The months that have come between
us, the miles that separated,
no longer distance us.
We are one beneath the same sun
on this lovely earth.
I have a gift for you:
a candle to burn on the
altar of your heart
this Christ mass, this Solstice,
this festival of light. . . .

Stephanie June Sorréll, b. 1956
English poet

CHRISTMAS IS CUMULATIVE. WHATEVER ELSE IT HAS LOST, EVERY YEAR WHICH HAS PASSED SINCE THE BIRTH OF CHRIST HAS RETAINED AND ADDED TO THE MAGIC OF LIGHT AND COLOR AGAINST A DARK BACKGROUND, TO THE HUMAN CAPACITY FOR APPRECIATION OF CHORDS AND BELLS AND MELODIES, TO THE SWEETNESS OF CHILDREN'S VOICES. . . .

Gladys Hasty Carroll, b. 1904
American writer

It will never never be gone, this Christmas or any other, because each is in my heart and my memory, and each has, a little, shaped me for the next.

FAITH BALDWIN (1893–1978)
AMERICAN WRITER

ILLUSTRATION ACKNOWLEDGMENTS

COVER: *Happy Christmas*, Viggo Johansen (Hirsch Sprungske Collection, Copenhagen and Bridgeman Art Library, London)

TITLE PAGE: *Poinsettia in a Blue and Gold Vase*, Albert Williams (N.E. Middleton)

p. 2: *Christmas Roses, Poinsettia, and Holly*, Albert Williams (N.E. Middleton)

p. 7: *Madonna and Child with Infant St. John the Baptist*, Francesco Granacci

p. 8: *Christmas Fruit and Nuts*, Eloise Harriet Stannard (Fine Art Photographic Library Limited)

p. 10: *And Winter's Breath Came Cold and Chill*, Joseph Farquharson

p. 13: *Poinsettia and Christmas Roses*, Albert Williams

p. 15: *Adoration of the Shepherds*, Louis Le Nain (The Trustees, The National Gallery, London)

p. 16: *Star of Hope*, Noel Syers (N.E. Middleton)

p. 19: *Christmas Dreams by the Fireside*, artist unknown (Fine Art Photographic Library Limited)

p. 21: *Christmas Treasures*, Brenda Burke

p. 23: *Christmas Magic*, Brenda Burke

p. 24: *The Sisters of Charity*, Charles Burton Barber (Beaton-Brown Fine Paintings, London and Bridgeman Art Library, London)

pp. 26–27: *A Warm Welcome*, Noel Syers (N.E. Middleton)

pp. 28–29 [detail]: *Christmas Eve*, George Bernard O'Neill (Fine Art Photographic Limited)

p. 30: *Happy Christmas*, Viggo Johansen (Hirsch Sprungske Collection, Copenhagen and Bridgeman Art Library, London)

p. 33: *A Family Occasion*, William Powell Frith RA (Harrogate Art Gallery)

p. 35 [detail]: *Christmas Morning*, Noel Syers (N.E. Middleton)

p. 37: *Christmas Dreams*, Brenda Burke

p. 39: *Children and Snowman*, John Hassall

p. 40 [detail]: *Robin and Snowdrops*, Charles Barker

p. 41: *Christmas Eve—Delivering Presents*, William Erasmus Jones (Fine Art Photographic Library Limited)

p. 42: *A New Light upon a Darkening World*, Vernon Ward

p. 45: *The Last Stage*, John Strevens

p. 47: *Victorian Santa*, artist unknown

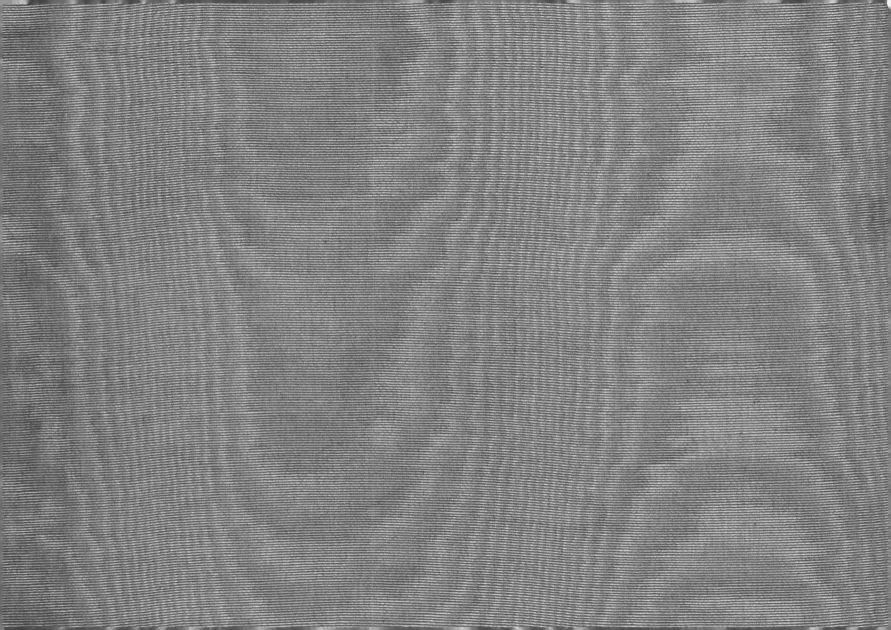